The Gruesome Truth About

The Tudors

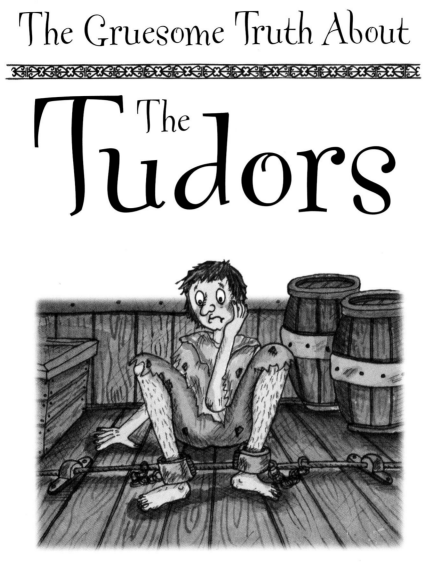

Written by

Jillian Powell

Illustrated by

Matt Buckingham

WAYLAND

First published in 2010 by Wayland

Text copyright © Wayland 2010
Illustration copyright © Matt Buckingham 2010

Wayland
338 Euston Road
London NW1 3BH

Wayland Australia
Level 17/207 Kent Street
Sydney NSW 2000

Editor: Victoria Brooker
Design: billybooks.co.uk
Consultant: Martyn Whittock, Head of History and
Director of Humanities Faculty, Kingdown School,
Warminster, Wiltshire.

British Library Cataloguing in Publication Data
Powell, Jillian
Gruesome truth about the Tudors.
1. Great Britain--History--Tudors, 1485-1603--Juvenile
literature. 2. Great Britain--Social life and customs--
16th century--Juvenile literature.
I. Title II. Tudors
942'.05-dc22

ISBN: 978 0 7502 6134 0

Printed in China

Wayland is a division of Hachette Children's Books,
an Hachette UK company.
www.hachette.co.uk

Contents

The Terrific Tudors   4

Tudor Grooming   6

Pongs and Pomanders   8

Spit-roasts and Sparrows   10

Cock fights and Cudgels   12

Cruel Classrooms   14

Scary Surgery   16

The Plague   18

Sailors and Explorers   20

Men and Muskets   22

Crime and Punishment   24

Terrible Tortures   26

Women and Witches   28

Glossary   30

Further Information   31

Illustrator Note   31

Index   32

Answers   32

The Terrific Tudors

The Tudors were a family of kings and queens who ruled England from 1485 to 1603. The Tudor age was a great time for new industries, education and explorers.

The Tudors gave us our first maps of Britain and the first atlases of the world.

▲ Falconry was a favourite sport of the Tudors.

They built magnificent palaces, mansions and the first theatres, called playhouses. It was a great age for the arts, including plays, poetry and music. William Shakespeare (1564 – 1616) the great English playwright was born in Tudor times.

▲ William Shakespeare's plays were performed at the Globe theatre.

During the 1500s, there were also important discoveries in science, that led to new inventions like the telescope and the microscope.

▶ King Henry VIII (1491 – 1547) is one of the most famous rulers of the Tudor period.

Gruesome truth

Those are some of the things that you probably already know about the Tudors, but in this book you'll find out the gory and grisly bits that no one ever tells you! Each double page will begin with a well-known FACT, before going on to tell you the **gruesome truth**. Look out for these features throughout the book – the answers are on page 32.

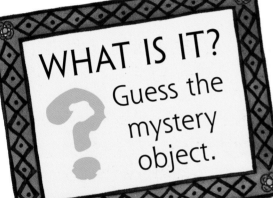

WHAT IS IT?
Guess the mystery object.

TRUE OR FALSE?
Decide if the statement is fact or fiction.

Age of Exploration

Explorers like Sir Walter Raleigh (1552 – 1618) and Sir Francis Drake (c.1540 – 1596) travelled overseas and brought back treasures and plants like potatoes and tobacco.

▶ Sir Francis Drake was the first Englishman to sail right around the world.

Tudor Grooming

FACT The Tudors wore beautiful clothes made from satin, silk and lace and used make-up, toothpaste and hair dyes.

Gruesome truth

In Tudor times, only royals and nobles were allowed to wear the richest fabrics and colours. Make-up often contained white lead, a deadly poison. It was sometimes used to hide the scars from smallpox and other diseases.

Bleach and belladonna

Pale skin showed that a woman came from a wealthy family and did not have to do rough outdoor work. To get a fair complexion, women bleached their skin with a mix of poisonous white lead and vinegar called 'ceruse'. They brushed this onto their face, neck and chest, then sometimes painted on blue veins to make their skin look finer. Some rich women were even bled to get a pale complexion. The doctor scratched or cut their skin then used a warm cup or leeches to suck out some blood.

▼ **Belladonna** drops dilated the pupils of the eye, but they could cause blurred vision and in time damage a person's eyesight.

Hair and wigs

Women used mercury sulphide (another poisonous chemical) or crushed cochineal beetles mixed with egg whites to redden their cheeks and lips. Hair was dyed red with henna, or yellow with saffron and cumin seeds or a mixture of sulphur and lead. The dyes sometimes made hair fall out and many people wore wigs.

▲ Queen Elizabeth I (1533 – 1603) was said to own 80 wigs.

Tudor teeth

The rich, including the royal family, often had rotten teeth because they ate lots of sweet, sugary foods that the poor could not afford. Some people tried to clean their teeth with honey, which only made them rot faster, but most used soot from a chimney, salt or chalk and chewed mint leaves to freshen their breath.

▲ Ordinary people sometimes painted their teeth black to get the same look as the royals and the rich.

TRUE OR FALSE?

The Tudors used toothpaste made from the heads of mice.

Pongs and Pomanders

FACT In Tudor times, people carried sweet-smelling flower posies and **pomanders** in their pockets. They even held small purses of herbs in front of their mouths as they spoke to sweeten their breath.

Gruesome truth

Posies and pomanders filled with herbs and spices were used to hide bad body odours and other smells. Some people believed that bathing too often was not good for the skin, or could even spread diseases like the Plague.

▼ Pomanders were stuffed with sweet-smelling herbs and spices and often worn hanging from belts

◄ Small posies of flowers were called nose-gays.

▲ Although Tudor toilets were called 'privies', they were not very private. Often they were just outside a back door and seated several people at a time.

Toilets and typhoid

Toilets were just wooden seats placed over a pot or hole in the ground. Some seated up to six people at a time. At Hampton Court palace, Henry VIII built a big common toilet for his courtiers, called 'The Great House of Easement'!

Poor people used moss or leaves instead of toilet paper and the rich used lambs' wool. Henry VIII had his own 'groom of the stool' whose job was to wipe his bottom clean! Open sewers carried sewage into **cesspits** or straight into rivers and streams. People used this water for cooking and washing clothes. Many people died from diseases like typhoid caused by dirty water.

Smelly streets

In Tudor towns and cities, people threw their rubbish into the street and emptied **chamber pots** out of windows. Streets smelled bad in the heat of the summer as rubbish and animal dung piled up.

▼ Women often wore shoes with wooden soles on iron rings to keep their feet above the filth in the streets.

WHAT IS IT?

9

Spit-roasts and Sparrows

FACT The Tudors enjoyed grand banquets with elaborate dishes of roast meats, pies and salads.

Gruesome truth

They ate everything from peacocks and porpoises to grilled beavers' tails, stewed sparrows, larks and robins.

Swans and spit-boys

Cooks competed to serve the grandest and most surprising dishes. Several birds were sometimes roasted together, stuffed one inside the other.

▲ A cockentrice was a roast made by sewing the front half of a chicken onto the back half of a pig, then roasting it in the oven.

▲ So many roast meats were served at royal banquets, that kitchens employed spit-boys whose job was to stand all day turning the handle of the spit-roast over the fire.

▼ Sometimes cooks baked a meat pie, took off the pastry lid and put small live birds inside. When the pie was cut at the table, the birds would fly out, giving guests an impressive show.

Spice and trenchers

Meat and fish was salted, spiced or pickled to store it over the winter months. Spices were also used for flavour. Food was served on wooden **trenchers**, or on thick slices of stale bread, which were then given to the poor or to the household dogs.

11

Cock fights and Cudgels

FACT The Tudors enjoyed a variety of games and sports including archery, falconry and jousting.

Gruesome truth

They also enjoyed cruel spectator sports like cock fighting and bear baiting.

Bulls, bears and bets

In the **bear gardens** of London, crowds would gather to watch trained dogs attack a bear or sometimes a bull that was chained to a post. Spectators would shout and jeer as they watched the animals fight to the death, placing bets on the outcome. Other animal 'sports' included watching a donkey attacked by a pack of dogs or a blinded bear being whipped by a group of men.

▲ Bears' teeth were clipped so the dogs were not killed immediately.

Cock fighting took place in pits and taverns. The birds were trained to fight and kill each other and people gambled on the winner.

◀ School boys were allowed to bring fighting cocks into school for a match once a year.

TRUE OR FALSE?
Footballs were made from pigs' bladders.

Football and fighting

In villages, men enjoyed football and cudgelling, a contest between two men fighting with thick sticks. There were no football pitches and few rules for the game. Men from rival villages kicked a ball between goal posts a mile or more apart.

▶ Football matches often ended in brawls, ambushes and fighting. Serious injuries like broken limbs were common.

Cruel Classrooms

FACT In Tudor times, boys from rich families were sent to school from the age of four, and learned subjects like Latin and Greek. The richest were educated by home tutors. Girls stayed at home and learned how to run a home.

Gruesome truth

Pupils who were naughty, or who didn't answer the teacher in Latin, would be beaten with a wooden rod or given 50 strokes of the birch. Sometimes teachers hit them across the mouth with a feral, a flat piece of wood with a hole on the top. Often boys ran away from school because they were so unhappy.

▶ Rich parents paid a 'whipping boy'. When their child was naughty, it was his whipping boy who got punished!

▲ Some children had to walk five or six miles every day to get to school.

Lousy lessons

Many school days started at 6 am and went on until 5 pm. Children only had Sundays off, and two holidays a year at Easter and Christmas. If they were lazy or could not understand their lessons, they were made to wear a Dunce's cap and stand or sit on a stool in the corner of the classroom.

TRUE OR FALSE?
School books were made of cow's horn.

◀ Children learned to write with quill pens, made from sharpened birds' feathers.

Scary Surgery

FACT In Tudor times, there were barber-surgeons, who worked as surgeons, barbers and dentists, and doctors and apothecaries, who made medicines and herbal cures.

Gruesome truth

Barber-surgeons sometimes had to do operations without any anaesthetic on soldiers wounded in battle, even drillling into skulls or removing limbs. In hospitals, the only anaesthetics were alcohol, **opium** or the poisonous plant hemlock.

▲ Assistants held the patient down while the barber-surgeon was operating.

Blood and oil

Surgeons wore their ordinary clothes for operations and just wiped instruments clean afterwards. They believed too much blood or bad blood would cause disease, so often they practised blood-letting, cutting or scratching the patient's skin, then using cups or leeches to suck out the blood. They used leeches, boiling oil or red-hot irons to clean wounds, but many patients died from infections or blood poisoning.

▼ 'Cupping' meant placing a warmed cup over a cut in the skin to draw out the blood.

Curious cures

Many people turned to herbal remedies or **superstitious** beliefs for cures. One cure for a headache was pressing a hangman's rope against the head. For baldness, they rubbed fat from a fox's body on the head. For **gout**, they boiled up a paste made from worms, pig's bone marrow and herbs with hair from a red-haired dog!

▲ To cure aches and pains in the joints, people were told to wear the skin of a donkey.

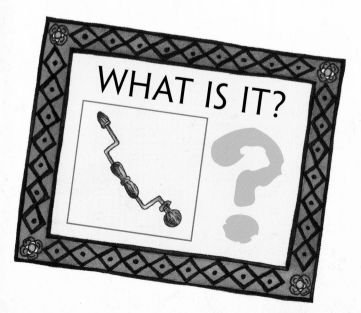

WHAT IS IT?

▲ Doctors used flasks to collect a patient's urine. They examined its colour and smell, and even tasted it to look for causes of illness!

The Plague

FACT In Tudor times, doctors believed that diseases like the Plague were spread by dirty air and smells. Many people believed they were a punishment from God for committing sins.

Gruesome truth

The Plague was a deadly disease that was spread by fleas that lived on rats. Poor hygiene in Tudor times meant that many people carried fleas or lice on their skin or hair. In 1563, nearly 2,000 people a week died from the Plague in London alone.

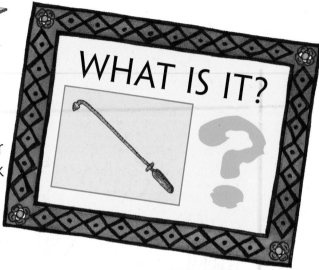

WHAT IS IT?

Bites and Buboes
People who caught the Bubonic Plague from a flea bite developed ugly black boils or buboes filled with pus on their armpits and lower body, vomited and coughed up blood. They could die within three days.

▼ Plague doctors wore long cloaks, leather hats and gloves. They carried sticks to keep patients away from them and wore masks that had beaks over the nose stuffed full of sweet smelling herbs.

▼ Red crosses were painted on doors and hand bells rung to warn of 'unclean' households where people were sick or dying. Sometimes dead bodies were left rotting inside until a death cart labourer carried them away at night on a hand cart. They were buried in mass graves called plague pits.

Sailors and Explorers

FACT The Tudors were great sailors and adventurers, travelling overseas to new lands to bring back new foods like cocoa, potatoes and apricots. John Cabot was the first European explorer to reach North America during the reign of King Henry VII (1457 – 1509).

Gruesome truth

Tudor ships were cramped and dirty and often infested with mice and rats. Sometimes over half the crew died of disease before the voyage was over.

Scurvy and weevils

Sailors lived on a diet of salted meat or fish and hard ship's biscuits that often contained **weevils** and maggots. They did not have fresh fruit or vegetables on board and often developed scurvy, a disease caused by a shortage of vitamin C. This caused blue-black spots on the skin, made their gums bleed and their teeth fall out. More sailors died from scurvy than from sea battles!

▶ Ship's biscuits were called 'hard tack'. They were so hard they had to be dunked in salty water to soften them.

▼ Sailors could fall from the masts and rigging. They had to climb rope ladders to adjust the sails even in stormy weather, without wearing any safety harness.

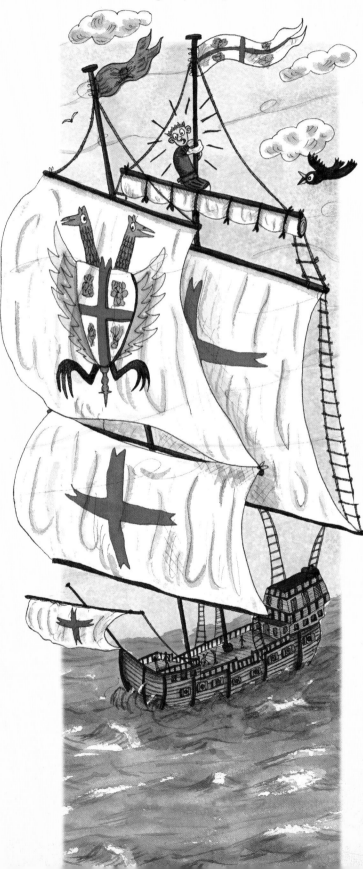

Cats and feathers

If a sailor was caught drunk or asleep on duty, he was given a flogging with a knotted rope called a cat o' nine tails, or 'put in irons'. Even harsher punishments were **tarring and feathering**, or tying sailors to a rope and ducking them overboard. Sometimes their bodies were dragged along under the ship. For the crime of murder or **mutiny**, a sailor was hanged from the arm of the ship's main sail.

▲ Sailors 'put in irons' were left below decks with their feet tied to an iron bar.

WHAT IS IT?

?

Men and Muskets

FACT Tudor armies fought with new firearms such as cannon guns and **muskets**.

Gruesome truth

Huge cannon guns made from bronze or iron fired stone or iron balls that could rip men to pieces. Some exploded in the faces of the gun crew who loaded them. Muskets fired round lead balls, much larger than bullets today, that caused terrible injuries.

▼ Gun crews loaded cannons with gunpowder and 'shot', or cannon balls. They also had to clean out the gun barrel and put water on it when it got too hot, otherwise it could explode.

Wicked weapons

Muskets were heavy guns nearly two metres long that had to be rested on forked sticks. Soldiers also fought with **pikes**, **bills**, swords and daggers that made deep flesh wounds. Longbows could fire more than ten arrows a minute, and the arrowheads had spikes that tore away flesh as they were pulled out.

▼ Tudor weapons included axes, lances, bills, longbows, pikes and muskets.

battle axe

musket

lance

longbow

Crafty captains

Tudor soldiers served in companies of around a hundred men, led by a captain. Pay and conditions were poor and more men died of the plague or other diseases than from fighting. Many captains were dishonest and carried on claiming pay for soldiers who had died.

Crime and Punishment

FACT The Tudors had no police force. Instead, Justices of the Peace kept law and order through law courts that ordered punishments for crimes like murder, theft and **vagrancy**.

Gruesome truth

Punishments included whipping, branding with hot irons and hanging.

▼ Public hangings had a carnival feel, with stalls selling pies and ale and **gallows** souvenirs.

Gory gallows

Hanging was used for crimes including theft, rebellion, riot and murder. The body was left to rot on the gallows as a warning to others. Murderers who had poisoned their victim could be boiled alive in hot lead or water.

▲ Many towns had a whipping post. People could be whipped just for stealing a loaf of bread.

▲ Criminals were often put in the **stocks** or **pillory** in a public place so people could jeer at them and pelt them with rotten eggs or tomatoes.

TRUE OR FALSE?
You could be put into the stocks for not wearing a hat on Sunday.

Beggars and brands

Hot irons were used to burn letters into a criminal's hand or cheek, such as T for thief or V for vagrant. Vagrants and beggars had a hole burned in their ear. If they were caught a second time, they had the other ear burned and a third time, they were hanged.

Terrible Tortures

FACT Tudor kings and queens used harsh punishments for serious crimes like murder and **treason**.

Gruesome truth

Terrible tortures were used to force prisoners to confess to a crime.

Tower terrors

Anyone accused of treason against the king or queen was thrown into the Tower of London to await execution. Many were hanged, drawn and quartered. They were hanged until half dead, then taken down and their body cut into quarters.

▶ For beheading, victims had their hands tied behind their back as they knelt with their head on the block and waited for the axe to fall.

Others were beheaded in a public place by an axe-man. Sometimes it took several attempts to get the axe through the neck and the axe-man had to finish the job with a saw. The heads were often stuck onto the spikes of London Bridge or other public buildings as a warning to others.

◀ In Tudor times, the Tower of London was used as a prison and place of torture.

The Rack

The Rack was a wooden frame with a roller at each end. The victim had their feet chained to one end and their wrists to the other. A handle was turned to tighten the chains around the rollers, stretching the victim's body until their limbs were pulled from their sockets.

◀ The Rack was used to try and get prisoners to confess to their crime. Each time they refused, the handle was turned.

▼ The Scavenger's Daughter was a metal frame that slowly squashed the victim's doubled-over body until blood came out of their nose and ears.

WHAT IS IT?

Women and Witches

FACT The Tudors were very superstitious and believed in witches and the **supernatural**. They thought witches could cause everything from a poor harvest to the Bubonic Plague.

Gruesome truth

Many women were accused of being a witch and were put on trial, then hanged, burned or drowned.

Terrible tests

It was mostly old women who lived alone who were accused. Some people even accused their own mothers or sisters! Women were given tests to prove their innocence. Some were put into sacks or had their arms tied to their sides and were thrown into a pond or river. Others were plunged into water on a ducking stool. If they floated, they were said to be a witch. If they sank, they were innocent, but often they drowned and died anyway.

▲ People were burned at the stake for being witches, or for refusing to accept the religion followed by the king or queen.

Moles and marks

Some men acted as 'witch finders' and were paid a fee for every witch they had hanged. Moles or birthmarks were sometimes called witch marks. One test was to prick the mark with a knife. If it didn't bleed, the woman was said to be a witch.

WHAT IS IT?

▲ A ducking stool was a chair tied to a frame that worked like a seesaw. As the frame arm was lifted, the chair was plunged into the water, often an icy cold pond or river.

Gossips and scolds

The ducking stool was also used to punish women for being gossips, or for talking too much or nagging their husbands. They could also be forced to wear a scold's bridle, a cage that went over their head with a spiked mouth plate that held down their tongue.

Glossary

apothecaries	Pharmacists who prepared medicines and herbal cures.
anaesthetic	A substance that causes temporary unconsciousness.
bear gardens	Public places in London that had an arena where crowds could watch animal sports like bear baiting.
belladonna	A poisonous plant from the nightshade family.
bill	A pole with a wide blade and sometimes hooks and spikes.
cesspits	Pits for sewage.
chamber pots	Pots used to wee in during the night.
gallows	A wooden frame used for hanging criminals.
gout	A disease that causes pain and swelling in joints, especially toes.
musket	A type of gun that fired lead balls.
mutiny	A rebellion by sailors against their officers.
opium	A drug from poppy flowers.
pike	A long spear.
pillory	A frame with holes for the head and hands that criminals were put into. The pillory was like stocks but meant standing up and was usually used for more serious crimes.
pomander	A small box or bag for carrying sweet smelling herbs.
stocks	A frame with holes for the feet and hands that criminals were put into, so they were held sitting down.
supernatural	Things that cannot be explained by science or the study of the natural world.
superstitious	Fears and beliefs not based on science or reason.
tarring and feathering	A punishment in which people are covered with hot tar and birds' feathers.
treason	The crime of trying to kill or harm the king or queen.
trencher	A dish or slice of bread that food is eaten off.
vagrant	Someone who is homeless and wanders from place to place.
weevil	A type of beetle.

Further Information

Books

A Tudor Medicine Chest (Inside Story) by Brian Moses, Wayland 2007

Tudor Medicine (Be a History Detective) by Dereen Taylor (Wayland, 2009)

Tudor War (Be a History Detective) by Katie Dicker (Wayland, 2009)

The Tudors (History Relived) by Cath Senker (Wayland, 2009)

The Terrible Tudors (Horrible Histories) by Terry Deary, Scholastic 2007

You Wouldn't want to be Ill in Tudor Times by Kathryn Senior, Wayland 2002

Websites

www.historyonthenet.com/Tudors/tudorsmain.htm

www.tudorhistory.org/topics

www.woodlands-junior.kent.sch.uk/Homework/Tudors.html

Places to visit

Hampton Court Palace, London
The Mary Rose, Portsmouth
Shakespeare's Globe theatre, Bankside, London
The Tower of London

Author Note

The Tudors were one of my favourite history topics when I was at school. I loved learning about their costumes and make-up, the houses they lived in and the foods they ate. I guess I knew a bit then about the more gruesome side of Tudor life, like people throwing their toilet waste out of the windows into the street, or catching the Plague from flea bites. But there was a lot more to learn about the terrible truths of Tudor lives.

Jillian Powell

Index

Numbers in **bold** refer
to illustrations.

banquets 10, **11**
battle 16
blood 6, 17, **17, 18, 27**
boys 12, 14, 14
Bubonic Plague, the 18, 28

children 15, **15**
clothes 6, 8
criminals 25, **25**

disease 6, 8, 17, 18, 20, 23
doctor 6, 16, **17**, 18, **18**

Elizabeth I, Queen **7**, 9
explorers 4, 5, 20-21

food 7, 11, 20

girls 14

Hampton Court Palace 8
hanging 24, **24**, 25, 26, 28
Henry VII, King 20
Henry VIII, King **4**, 8
hospitals 16

leeches 6, 17

make-up 6
men 22, 29

Plague, the 8, 18-19, **18**,
  23
plants 5, 16
poison 6
poor 11
punishment 18, 21, 24-25,
  26

religion **28**
rich 6, 7, 7, 8, 14, **14**

sailors 20-21, **21**
school **12**, 14, 15, **15**
scurvy 20
sewage 8
Shakespeare, William 4, **4**
soldiers 16, 23
sport **4**, 12

teacher 14
teeth 7, 7
theatres 4, **4**
toilets 8, **8**

weapons 23, **23**
witches 28-29, **28**
women 6, 7, 9, 28-29
work 6

 # Answers

Page 7 True. The heads of mice were ground up to make toothpaste.

Page 9 Probably false. Queen Elizabeth I may have taken baths more often than most as she had piped water in some of her palaces and took portable baths with her when travelling.

Page 9 A bone ear scoop, used for cleaning wax out of the ears.

Page 13 True. Pigs' bladders were filled with peas and used as balls.

Page 15 False, but pupils did use hornbooks which were wooden boards with a handle that had Christian prayers on one side and the alphabet on the other. The paper on them was covered with a thin layer of cow's horn.

Page 17 What is it? A trepan, used to drill holes into a patient's skull to cure headaches.

Page 18 A plague cautery. Doctors used this long-handled tool to burst buboes without getting too near the patient.

Page 21 A cat o' nine tails, a leather whip used for flogging sailors.

Page 25 True. Everyone had to cover their head on the holy day of the week, Sunday.

Page 27 Thumb screws. They were gradually tightened around the victim's thumbs to torture them.

Page 29 The 'brank' or scold's bridle.

The Gruesome Truth About

Contents of titles in the series:

The Middle Ages
978 0 7502 6133 3

The Marvellous Middle Ages
Dingy Dwellings
Herbs and hygiene
Weary workers
Working children
Boars and bustards
Hunting and hawks
Castles and Catapults
Sheriffs and Stocks
Terrible tortures
Deadly diseases
Curious cures
Prayers and Pardons

The Tudors
978 0 7502 6134 0

The Terrific Tudors
Tudor Grooming
Pongs and Pomanders
Spit roasts and sparrows
Cock fights and cudgels
Cruel classrooms
Scary Surgery
The Plague
Sailors and Explorers
Men and Muskets
Crime and Punishment
Terrible Tortures
Women and Witches

The Victorians
978 0 7502 6135 7

The Vivacious Victorians
Homes and Hygiene
Cruel Rules
Dodgy Dinners
Dunce Caps and Canes
Arsenic and Leeches
'The Great Stink'
Pickpockets and Pudding Snammers
Hulks and Hangings
Foul Factories and Monstrous Mills
Chimneys and Coalmines
Boxing and Baiting
Freaks and Acrobats

The Vikings
978 0 7502 6132 6

The Valiant Vikings
Ruthless Raiders
Wild Warriors
Sacrifices and Sagas
Chieftains and Slaves
Laws and 'Things'
Families and Feuds
Smoky Homes
Soap and Steam Baths
Horrid Hunters
Seabirds and Sausages
Cruel Competitors
Pyres, Fires and Funerals

WAYLAND

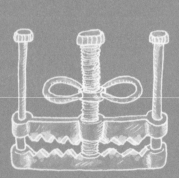